PIXEL PLANET
SECTION 1:
ANIMALS

D0470677

Snoozy Suzie

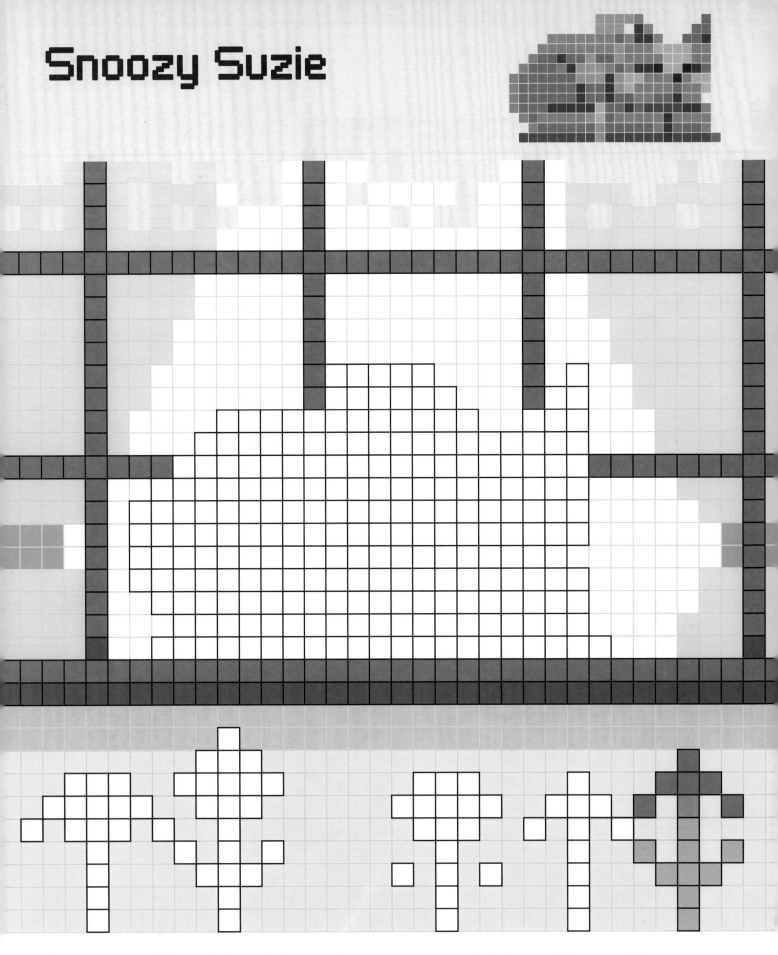

I'm a pretty kitty with soft fur and a gorgeous pink bow. I like nothing better than having a catnap on the sunny windowsill...purrrfect!

Playful Patch

I'm just a playful dog, always wagging my tail. When I see my favorite ball, I run around the backyard and bark. Woof, woof!

Buddy Birdsong

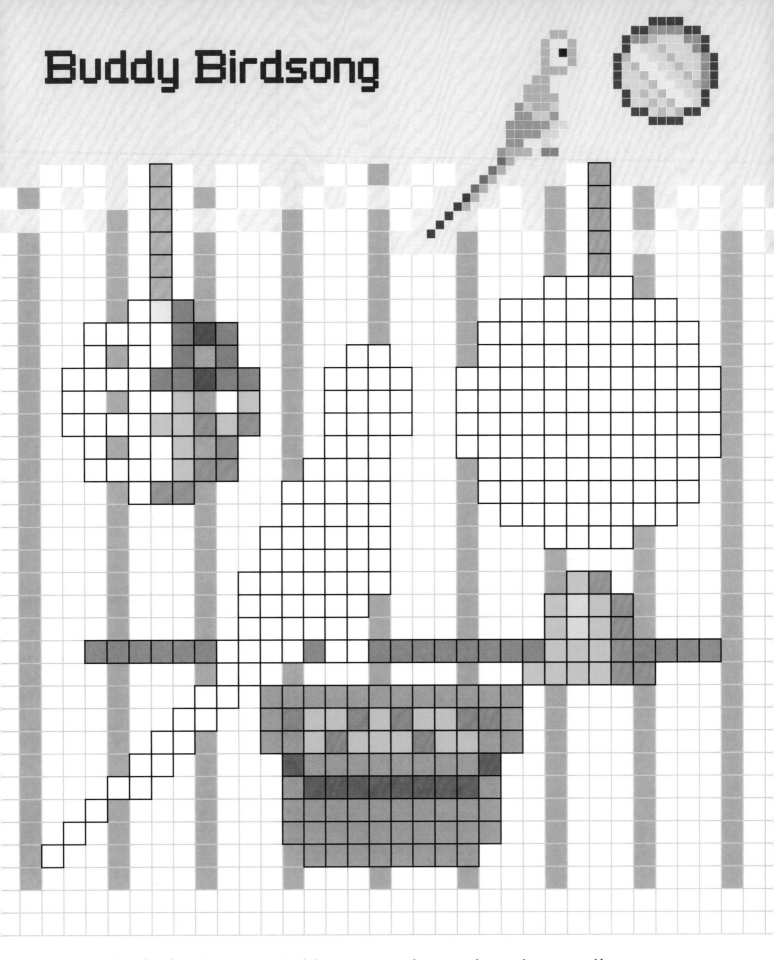

I'm a colorful budgerigar and I preen and stretch and tweet. I'm a pretty boy and I love looking at myself in the mirror...chirp, chirp, chirp!

Fab Fish!

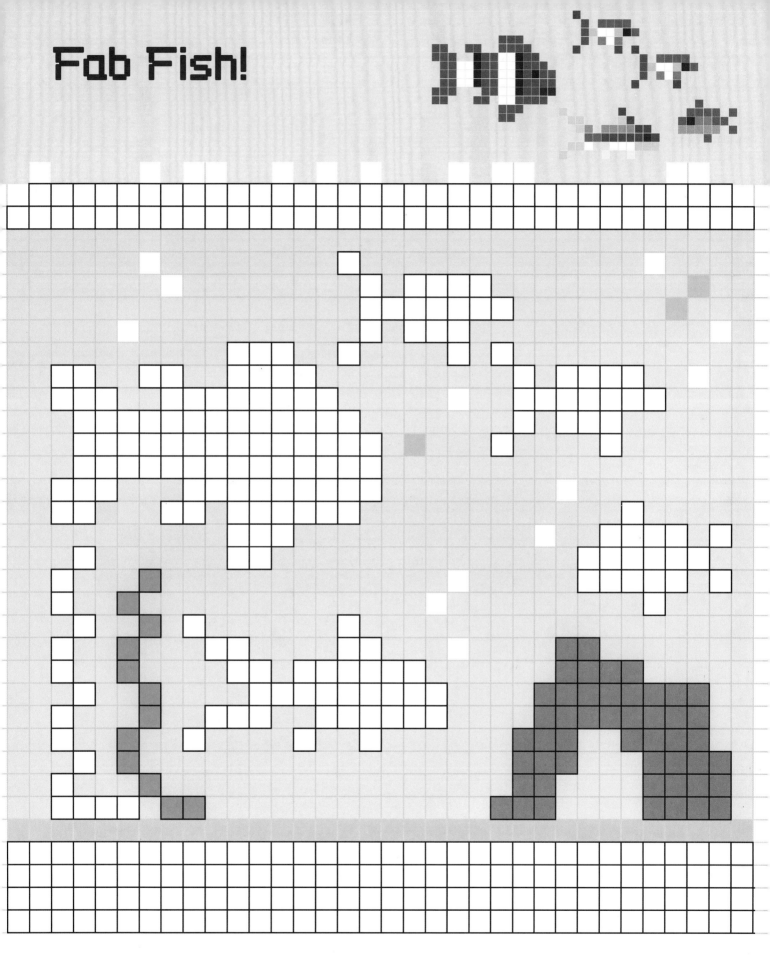

We are colorful fish of all shapes and sizes. We love hiding amongst the plants and rocks in our tank...bloop, bloop, bloop!

Nippy Nora

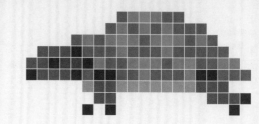

I'm a slippery terrapin and I love swimming in the water and sunning myself on a rock. Don't get your fingers too close. Snap!

Flopsie

I'm just a happy bunny rabbit and I love hopping around the backyard.
I get very excited when I see my favorite food...carrots!

Dear Ducks!

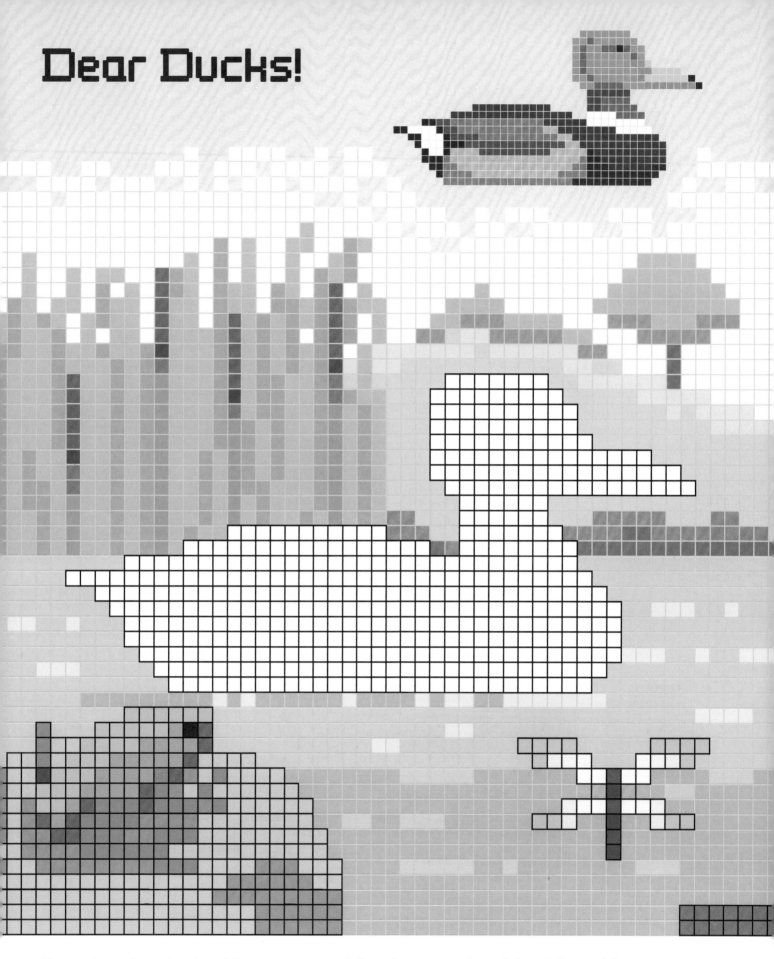

I'm a hungry duck with waterproof feathers and webbed feet. I love to preen my feathers to keep them shiny and clean.

We are little ducklings. We swim, swim, swim...looking for tasty plants and insects to eat. Peep, peep, peep!

Chatty Gabby

I'm a happy, chatty guinea pig and I nibble grass all day. I love crunchy fruit and vegetables as a very special treat. Yum!

Hungry Henry

I'm a lucky little hamster because I can store food in my stretchy cheeks.
I like to sleep during the day. At night I wake up and play! Squeak!

Chirpy Chicks

We are bundles of yellow feathery fun. Cheep, cheep, cheep! We won't
stay like this for long, because we grow up very fast!

Lazy Daisy

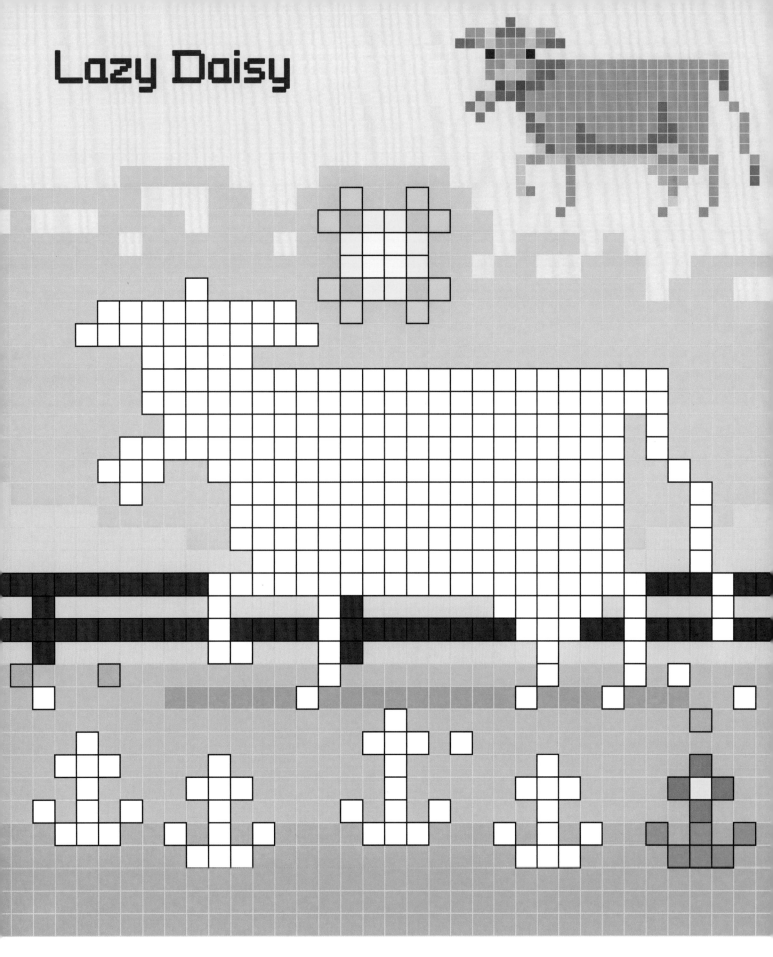

I'm a friendly cow and I munch grass all day. I give you milk for drinking—and making butter, cheese, and yogurt too.

Monty Mouse

I'm a pet mouse and I scurry and play in my cage. I love dawn and dusk, when I get up to mousy mischief! Squeak, squeak!

Field Mouse Family

We are a family of field mice. We live outdoors and hunt for yummy food like snails, seeds, and insects!

Fishy Friends

I'm Fancy Fifi, the biggest, prettiest fish in the aquarium. Just look at my fancy colors and patterns. Pretty me!

We are more pretty fish! We love swimming in the clear water, having fun with our fishy friends.

Dilly Dachshund

I'm a playful little hound with a long body and very short legs. I run to keep up with my owner when we go for walks. I have lots of energy!

Bouncy Benji

I'm a bouncy, yappy puppy dog. When I'm not chasing a ball, I'm busy chasing my tail! Yap, yap!

Nutty Nancy

I'm a busy little squirrel and I'm nuts about nuts! I sometimes bury them to keep them safe. Now where did I hide the last one?

Foxy Felix

I'm such a handsome fox, with my big, bushy tail! I live in a beautiful park, close to town, where I hide in the daytime.

Penguin Pastimes

I'm a big daddy penguin with a very important job. I'm keeping an egg warm until my chick is ready to hatch. Peck, peck, peck!

We are happy penguin chicks, slipping, sliding, and skidding in the ice and snow. Wheeeee!

Eight-arms Amy

I'm an amazing octopus with eight wiggly, squiggly arms. I can hide by changing color to match my background. That's cool!

Snappy Stanley

I'm a snippety-snappety crab with clickety-clackety claws! I scuttle around the seashore, but I love rock pools best of all. Snip, snap!

Dolphin Friends

We are sleek and graceful dolphins. In and out of the waves we swim, hunting for fish and squid. Splish, splash, splosh!

We are all great friends! We love to spend time together, diving, splashing, and having fun!

Croaking Cuthbert

I'm a hungry green frog. I sit still on my lily pad, keeping a lookout for yummy flies. Croak, croak, croak!

Dainty Dora

I'm a shy little deer with a soft, velvety coat. I tiptoe through the trees nibbling grass, shoots, and leaves.

Slithering Sam

I'm a slithering, hissing snake. I glide through the forest, hunting for lizards, eggs, and frogs...and I swallow them whole! Gulp!

Toothy Terence

I'm a grinning crocodile with a mouth full of teeth. But beware of my smile, because I'm feeling hungry! SNAP!

Timmy Toucan

I'm a talkative toucan with an enormous colorful bill. It's perfect for reaching all the tasty fruit I like to eat.

Polly Parrot

I'm just a pretty parrot and I love to make a noise. I screech and squawk all day. Look at me! Look at me!

Climbing Milo

I'm a fun-loving monkey with a very useful tail. It's awesome for climbing and swinging through the trees!

Gorgeous George

I'm a gorgeous gorilla—a very special beast. There aren't many of us left, so it's important for me to stay safe.

Enormous Ellie

I'm an enormous elephant with a super-amazing trunk. I use it for breathing, drinking, and holding things. Lucky me!

Towering Twins

We are giraffes—the tallest land animals in the whole world! We love the tastiest leaves from the highest trees. Munch, munch, munch!

Bright Butterflies

We are fluttering butterflies with beautiful, colorful wings. We fly from flower to flower, looking for sweet nectar to eat.

We love the warm summer sun and backyards full of pretty summer
flowers. Aren't we lovely?

Pink Patsy

I'm a pretty flamingo with pink feathers, and a long neck and legs. I wade in shallow water, scooping up food with my big bill.

Roaring Rex

I'm a big wild cat with an amazing furry mane. I hunt other animals and I have a very loud voice. Rooaaar!

Soaring Sidney

I'm a powerful bird of prey with big wings and excellent eyesight. I soar high in the sky, looking out for my next meal. Watch out below!

Hooting Harry

I'm a feathery owl and I come out at night. I love hunting in the moonlight, when you're fast asleep! Hoo-hoo!

Brilliant Bugs

I'm a red and black ladybug, so I'm easy to see! You'll find me crawling around the backyard and even hiding indoors!

We are more creepy-crawlies. You'll find us hiding in all kinds of places.
Spot us if you can!

Slow Seymour

I'm a slimy snail with my house on my back. I take life slowly as I crawl along, and I hide in my shell to keep safe.

Hopping Hattie

I'm a bouncy kangaroo with powerful legs and a long tail. I keep my baby safe in my pouch while he grows. Boing, boing, boing!

Humpy Hugo

I'm a big desert animal with a hump on my back. I can go without water for a long time, which is great for living in hot places!

PIXEL PLANET

SECTION 2:
DINOSAURS
AND OTHER PREHISTORIC
CREATURES

Triceratops

This plant-eating dinosaur's name means "three horned face."
It had an impressive bony frill around its neck too!

Ankylosaurus

Ankylosaurus was covered in protective spikes and plates of bone.
Predators had to watch out for its powerful clubbed tail!

Herd Behavior

Triceratops lived in herds, just like cattle do today. Young Triceratops were kept in the middle of the herd to protect them from predators.

Brachiosaurus

The enormous, plant-eating Brachiosaurus reached 82 feet in length!
It had a long tail and neck, and nostrils on the top of its head.

Giganotosaurus

This fearsome predator weighed more than a T. rex and had enormous jaws, packed with razor-sharp teeth!

Feeding Time

With their incredibly long necks, this herd of Brachiosaurus are munching leaves from the tops of the trees.

Parasaurolophus

This dinosaur had a long hollow crest at the back of its head. The crest may have been used to make loud noises to other members of the herd.

Protoceratops

This plant-eater had a parrot-like beak and a large bony head frill. It was only about 6 feet long—snack size for a hungry theropod!

Spinosaurus

With a distinctive sail on its back, Spinosaurus is one of the largest known carnivorous (meat-eating) dinosaurs.

Stegosaurus

Easily recognizable by the plates on its back and its spiked tail, this giant armored dinosaur had a tiny brain for its size.

Looking for Food

Stegosaurus were about the same size as a modern bus!

They needed to eat a lot of plants, such as mosses, ferns, horsetails, and conifers in order to survive.

Tyrannosaurus rex

The "king of the tyrant reptiles" had teeth like steak knives and a bite that was three times more powerful than a modern lion's!

Hadrosaur

This duck-billed dinosaur had loads of teeth and a hinged jaw that helped it to grind up huge quantities of vegetation.

T. rex Attack!

These hadrosaurs are looking for some nice plants to eat. Little do they suspect that it could be their last meal!

Graciliceratops

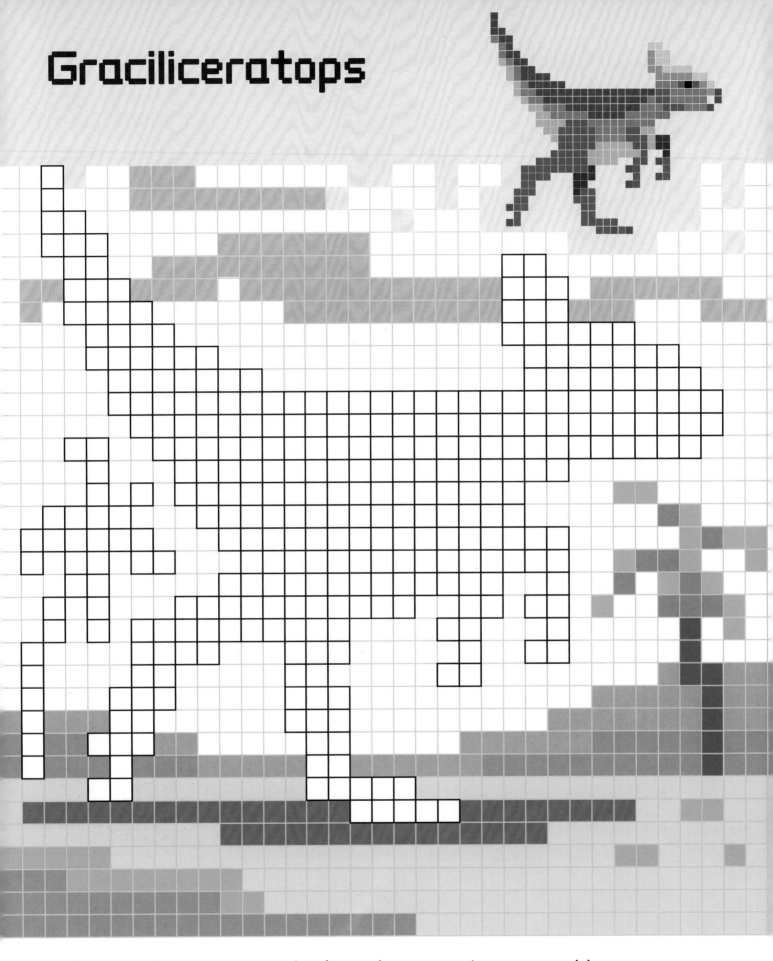

This small dinosaur was only about the same size as a cat! Its name means "graceful horned face."

Diplodocus

At 90 feet in length, this giant herbivore had a long neck and a whip-like tail. Diplodocus swallowed stones to help grind up plants in its stomach.

Pachycephalosaurus

Pachycephalosaurus butted heads when competing with rivals. It's just as well they had a thick bony skull to protect their brain!

Archaeopteryx

This small, feathered dinosaur had sharp teeth and a killing claw. Scientists think it may be the link between dinosaurs and modern birds.

Jurassic Skies

Archaeopteryx probably weren't the best fliers, but they could take flight and glide to escape from trouble and to look for prey.

Scutellosaurus

Scutellosaurus means "little-shielded lizard." It is one of the earliest known armored dinosaurs.

Deinonychus

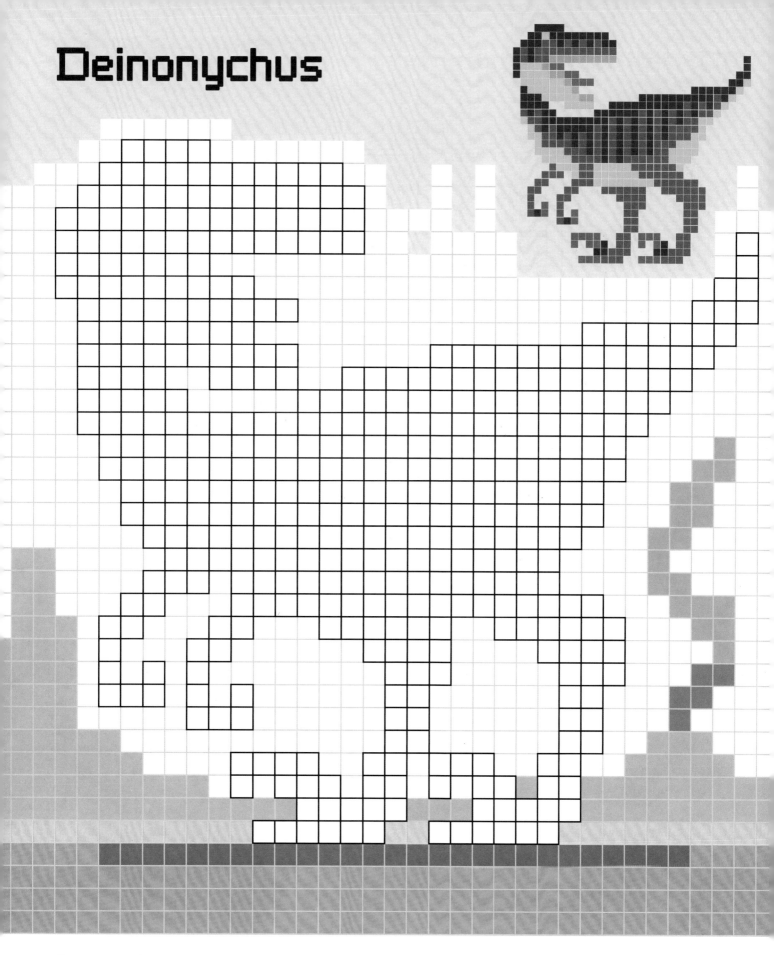

Deinonychus were quite small compared to other carnivores at the time, but they were ferocious hunters!

Pack Hunters

Deinonychus had a retractable killing claw on each foot and hunted in packs for much larger prey. Their name means "terrible claw!"

Kronosaurus

Kronosaurus was a marine reptile that lived at the time of the dinosaurs. It fed on turtles and plesiosaurs and was a very formidable predator!

Mosasaurus

Mosasaurus belonged to the "sea lizard" family and used its powerful tail, paddle-like limbs, and sharp teeth to hunt fish close to the water's surface.

Marine Predator

The thick-bodied aquatic Mosasaurus could devour an entire school of fish in a single mouthful, and could reach 59 feet in length!

Shonisaurus

At 52 feet long and weighing 33 tons, the Shonisaurus was one of the largest animals to ever inhabit Earth.

Quetzalcoatlus

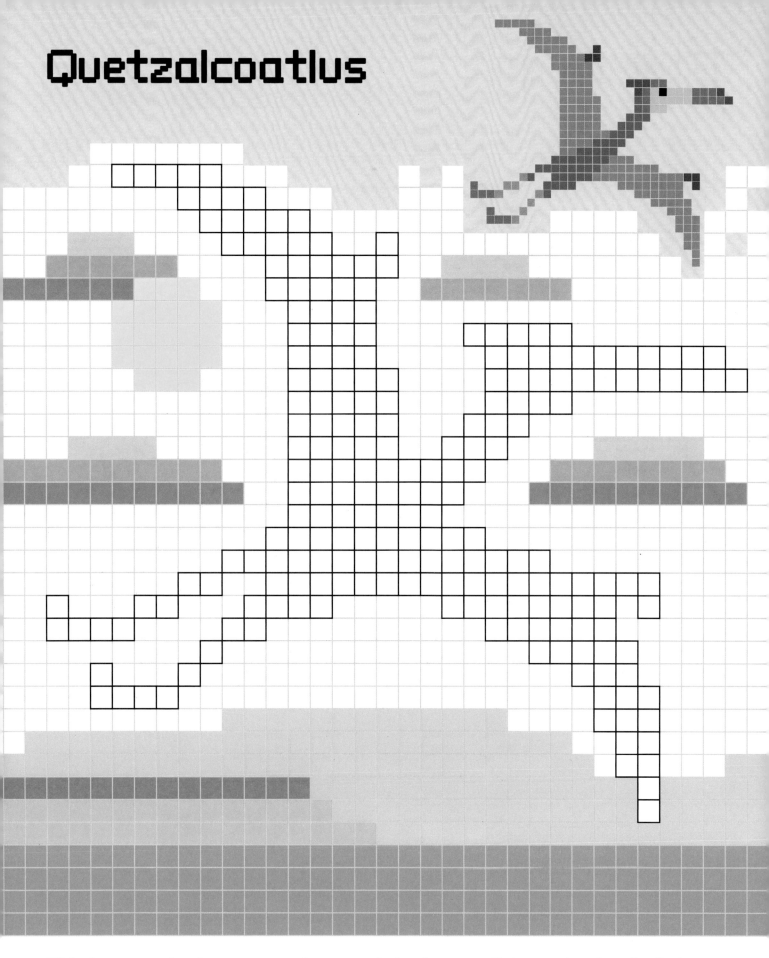

This long-necked pterosaur is one of the largest flying animals of all-time.
It had a mighty wingspan of 36 feet!

Pteranodon

The Pteranodon was a master at catching fish in its beak and then eating them whole! It had no teeth and its name means "toothless flier."

Dimetrodon

Dimetrodon walked the Earth 40 million years before the first dinosaurs and is actually more closely related to mammals than dinosaurs!

Saber-Toothed Cat

With their saber-like canine teeth, these ferocious carnivores preyed on large mammals like elephants and rhinos up until 11,000 years ago.

Giant Bear

The Giant Short-Faced Bear was one of the scariest predators of the Pleistocene. Adults could rear up to 13 feet high and run 35 mph!

Megalodon

The Megalodon was one of the most powerful predators ever! With massive teeth, immense size and powerful jaws, even whales were its prey.

Dunkleosteus

Long before dinosaurs evolved, this heavily-armored 32-feet long fish swam the oceans looking for prey.

Monster Shark!

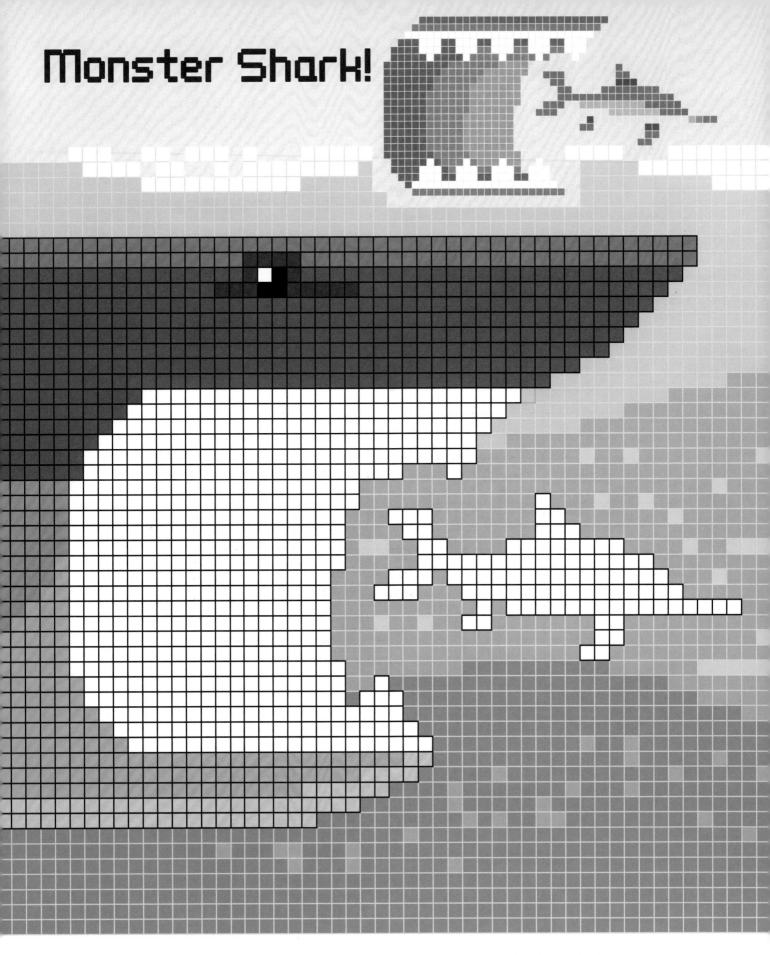

The Megalodon was the top predator in the oceans before it became extinct. Entire species migrated away from the areas it inhabited!

Ammonites

Ammonites are an extinct group of marine animals. Fossils of this creature's distinctive spiral-shaped shell can be found all over the world.

Dire Wolf

The extinct dire wolf was considerably larger than modern-day gray wolves and had bigger teeth! Like modern wolves and dogs, they hunted in packs.

Woolly Mammoth

The woolly mammoth was roughly the size of a modern African elephant, but with bigger tusks. It had thick, shaggy hair to protect it from the cold.

Woolly Rhino

Slightly larger than a modern-day white rhino, this extinct species had thick, long fur to keep it warm in the cold, icy territories it inhabited.

PIXEL PLANET
SECTION 3:
PEOPLE

Dusty Stetson

I'm a fast-shootin' rancher from the old Wild West. I'm as tough as old boots and quicker than a rattlesnake! Yee-hah!

Stumpy McPatch

I'm a swashbucklin' pirate with one eye and one leg. I sail the seven seas in search of gold doubloons. Aaaargh!

Pharaoh Nuff

I'm the greatest pharaoh that has ever ruled Ancient Egypt. My hobbies include building sandcastles and taking my pet lion for walks. Good kitty!

Max Speed

That's one small step for man, one giant leap for pixelkind!

Luke Out

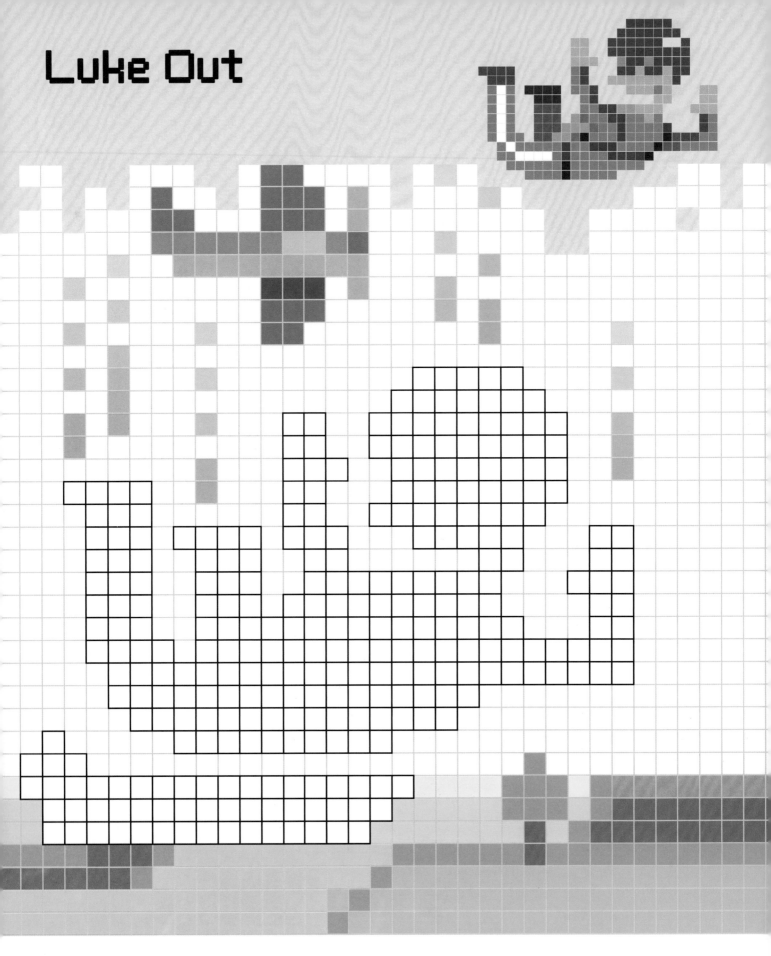

Sky diving is so much fun. Wait a minute, where's my parachute?

Mr. R. Otting

I used to be alive, but now I am a walking dead monster who loves to eat humans! Munch!

The Red Devil

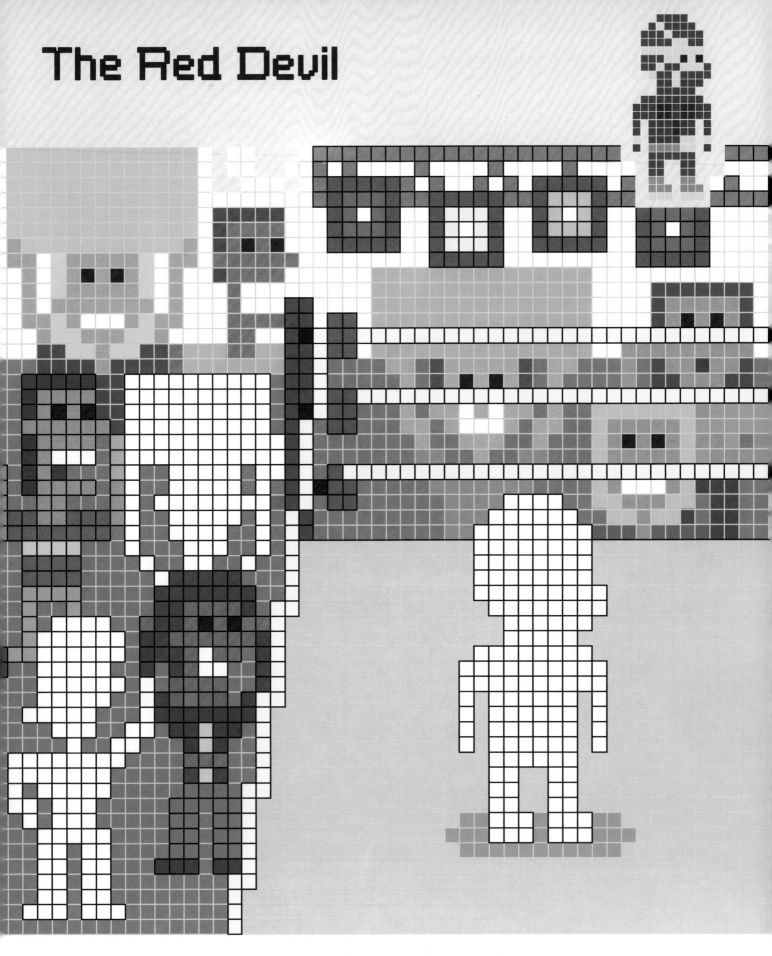

I, the Red Devil, have sworn to defeat my ultimate foe in one-on-one combat! Ha, ha, ha, ha!

The Masked Avenger

You will never defeat me, for I, the Masked Avenger, am the greatest wrestler ever! No really, I am, you can ask my mom.

Nick Money

Hands up! Your bunny or your life! I mean my life or your honey!
I mean...oh forget it.

Rod Steel

Between you and me, could you color me in some bigger muscles?

Mel Odey

This next song is going out to the intelligent, good-looking kid with the pencils. That's you, dummy!

Count Sheep

I'm a blood-sucking vampire with a sleep problem. Well have you tried sleeping in the daytime?

Sue Perkid

I use my superpowers to fight crime and protect the innocent. Watch out, bad guys, here I come! Kapow!

Rusty Bolt

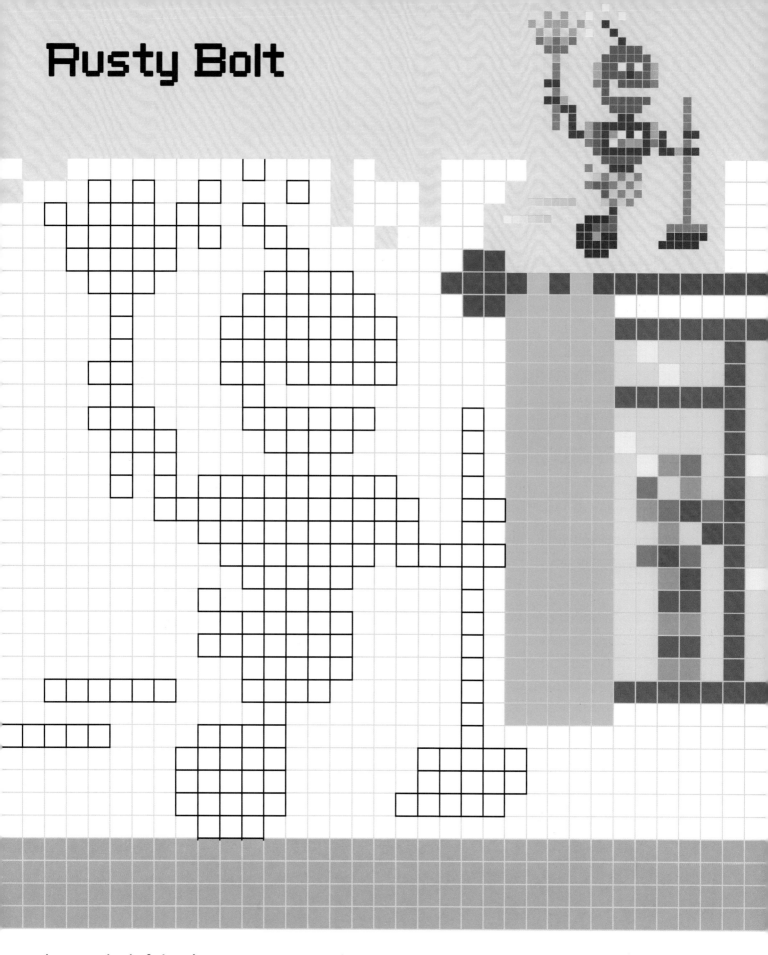

I am a helpful robot programmed to do all the jobs you don't want to.
I love tidying up, and doing homework. Beep beep!

King George the Quite Good

I'm the king, so everyone has to do what I tell them to. Now color me in—and that's an order!

Queen Alice

I wish I'd married King Charles the Great. No one takes a "quite good" king seriously. Sigh...

Jock Power

I'm the star quarterback of the team. Hut, hut, hike!

Master Piece

Hello! I am a very famous painter. I would like to paint you.
Your face is very strange and interesting.

Victoria de Boulderdash

I'm a princess and I live in a huge palace, full of old things. It's so boring!
I love ponies, flowers, and sparkly tiaras. Ding-a-ling-aling—it's teatime!

Chuck Danger

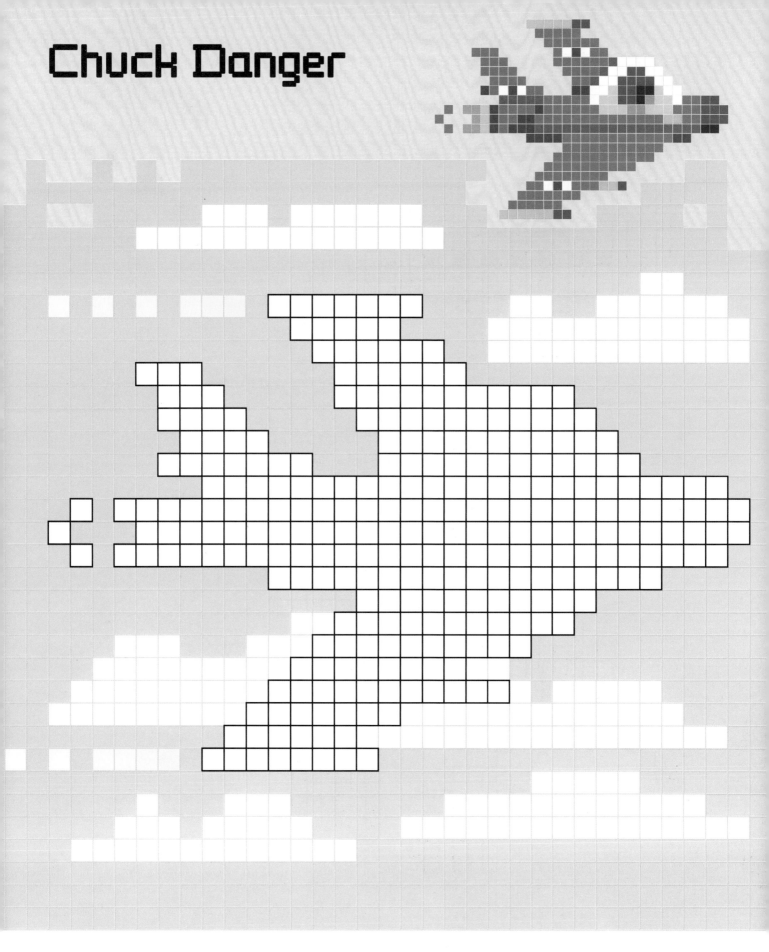

Hey, Chuck Danger here. I'm a fighter pilot. I feel the need, the need for speed! Vroom!

Serge Up

I am the world's most famous climber, and I have climbed all the highest peaks and most dangerous mountains.

Sherpa Sum Mit

I have climbed them all too!

Plenty O'Bubbles

Blub blub blub. Blub blub blub, blub, blub blub. Blub blub blub blub blub!

Mr. S. P. Ells

Stand back! I'm about to summon my breakfast. Toastandjamio!

Erik the Angry

My favorite things are raiding, plundering, fighting, and kittens.
WHAT'S SO FUNNY?

Maximus Pugnacius

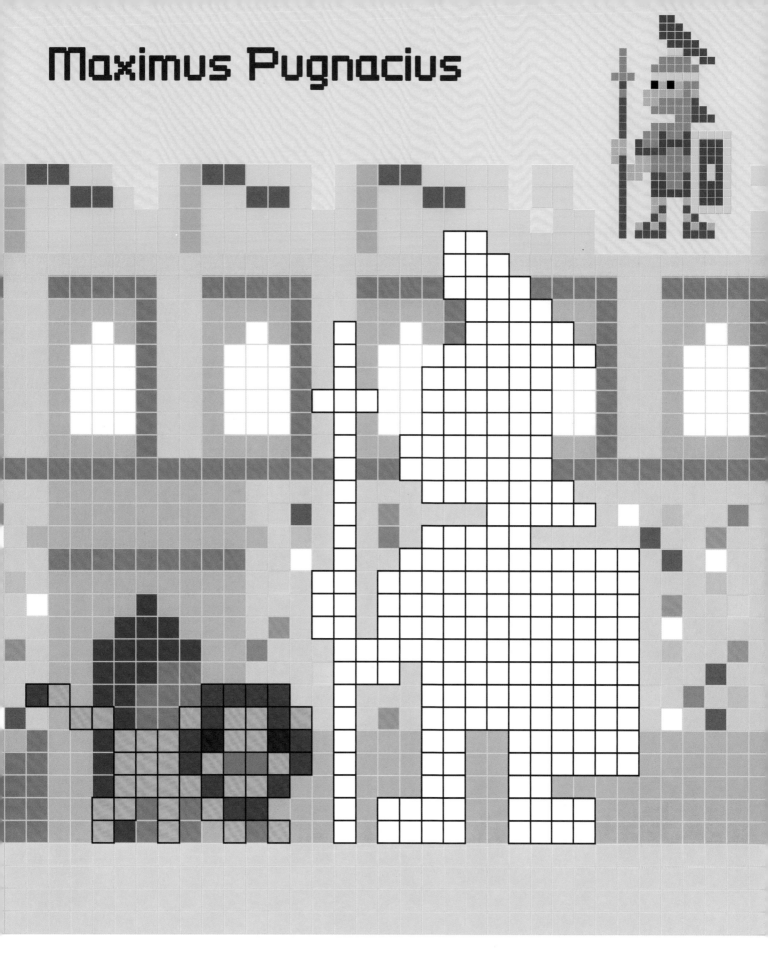

The Roman army is famous for its discipline. We always tidy up
after fighting.

Hairy Styles

When the full moon rises something terrible happens.
Don't get too close, I bite!

Anne Teak

I've been sleeping for thousands of years. Now someone has woken me up...and I'm not very happy!

Rob A. House

I'm just borrowing this...don't tell anybody.

Miss N. Chanter

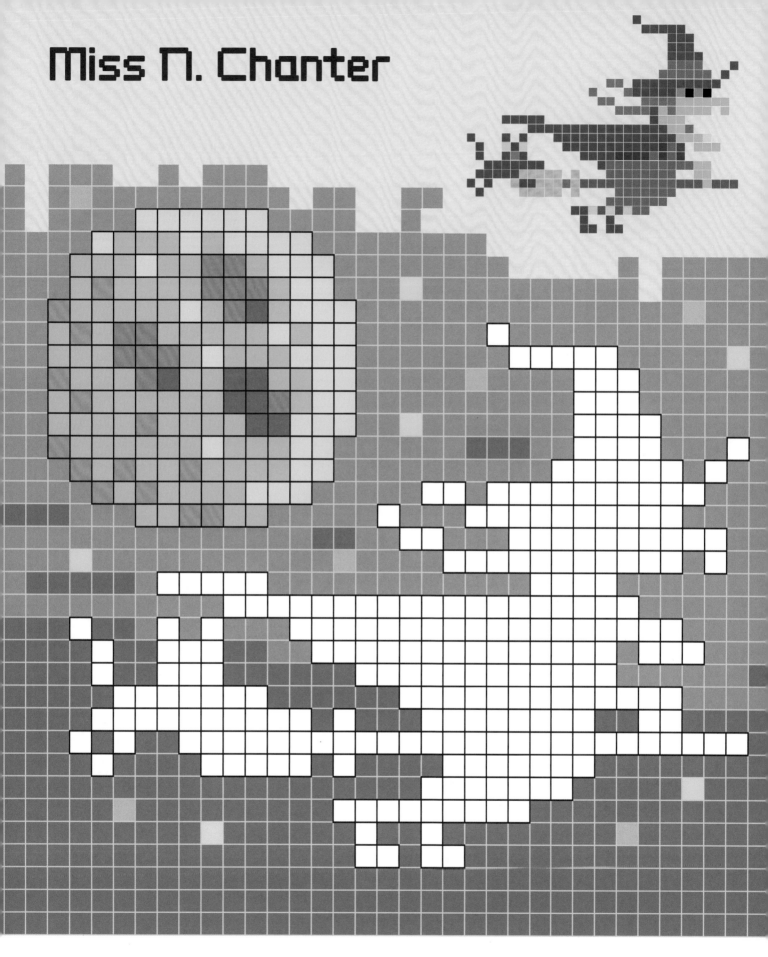

You don't want to mess with me. I once turned a tadpole into a frog!

Tommy Rocket

Hey everybody, put on your leather pants and get ready to rock out!
Tommy Rocket is here to party!

Jeet Kun Who

I am a deadly ninja and can move invisibly. You can see me? Umm...

Sir Lee

I'm a bad tempered knight from days of old. I love to fight and I'm the best jouster in the kingdom!

Sir Prise

Ha! I'll show you who's the best, you scoundrel! I challenge you to a pixel joust!

The Incredible Ian

I already know how to saw a person in half. Next week I'm learning how to put them back together again.

Captain Joe

Soldiers sing when they run,
Pixel Pix is really fun!

Ray Sing

I'm about to jump this here canyon on ma' bike. It looks bigger than I thought it was. Gulp!

Mike At

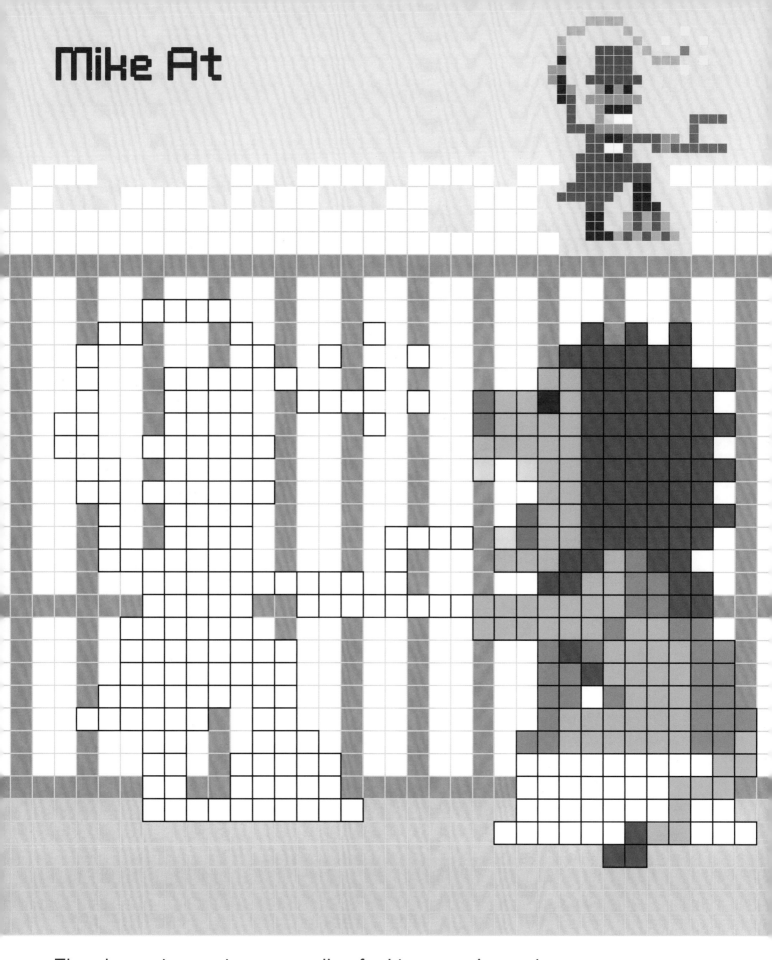

The clowns in my circus are all safe. Lions won't eat them.
They taste funny!

Dr. Chop

Don't worry, I've seen this operation before in a movie.

Nurse Worse

It's hard work being a nurse! There's always lots of people to help.
Um, are you sure that's right, Doctor?

Eva Searching

I've been exploring this jungle for over five years. Actually, this is a bit embarrassing, but I'm completely lost!

Cave Man

Ugg ugg. Ugg ugg ugg ugg uggg uggggg!

Yaron Mars

My squadron has been scrambled. There's an alien invasion!

Arthur Brick

I can build you a house, no problem. I just need some help coloring it in!

Hugh Mongous

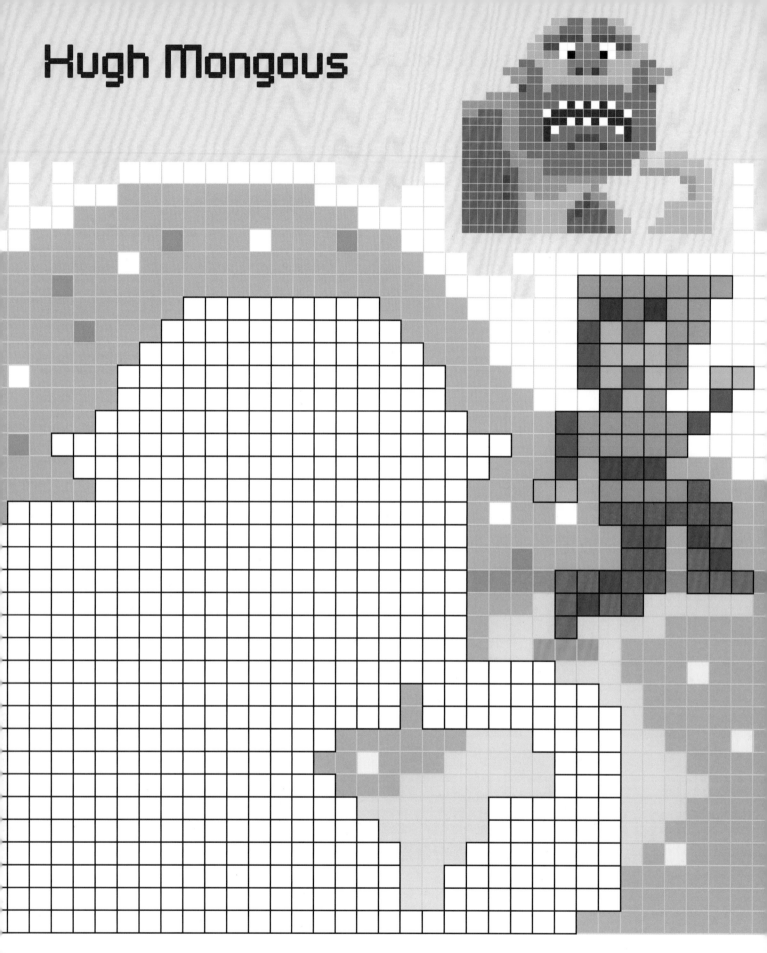

I'm a friendly giant, but every time I meet someone new they run away screaming. Will you be my friend?

PIXEL PLANET
SECTION 4:
SPACE ADVENTURE

Spaceship "Quantum"

This spaceship is the pride of the Galactic Empire. Its mighty engines blast it through space at light speed! Whoosh!

Speeder

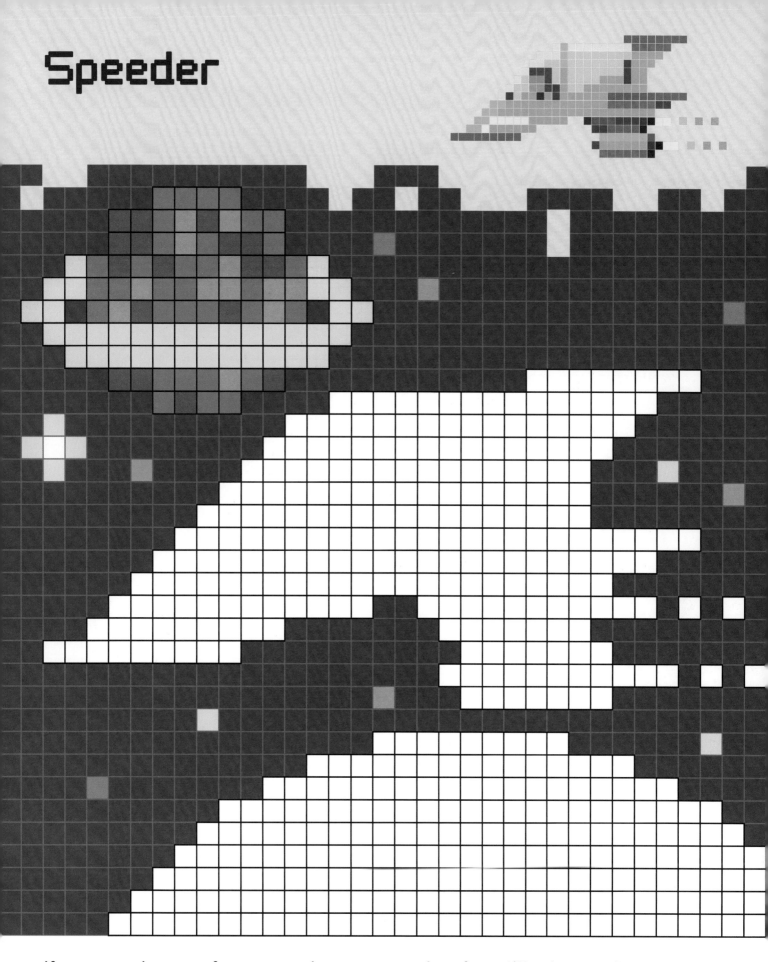

If you need to get from one planet to another fast, I'll take you in my speeder, but it will cost you! Hold on tight!

Mine Craft

These awesome mining machines travel the outer galaxy in search of precious metals and minerals. Start the drills!

Battleship

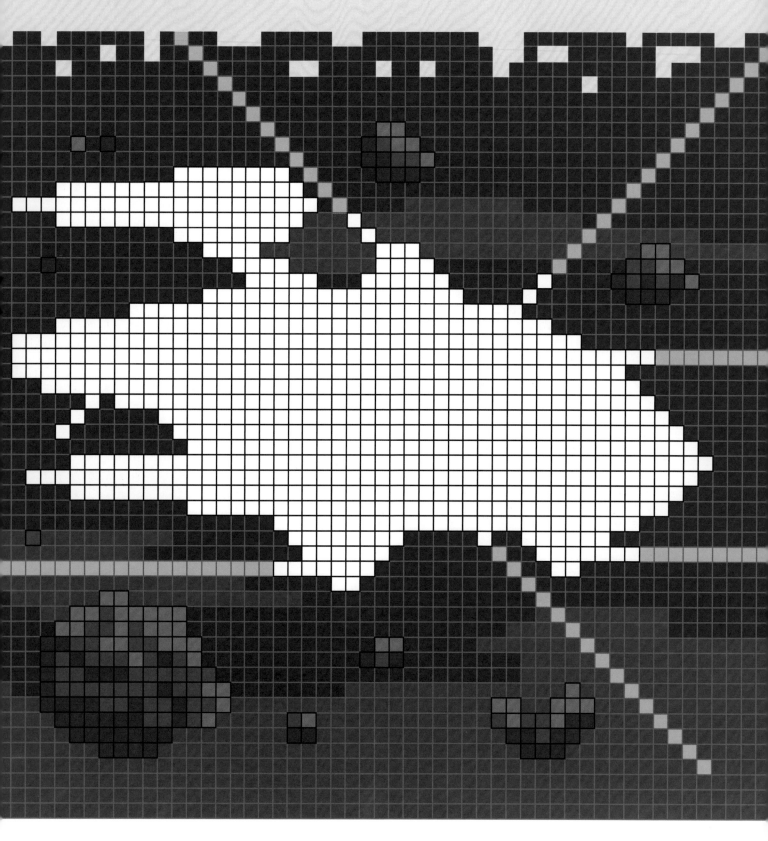

This battleship is state-of-the-art. It's testing out its new pulsar cannons on some passing asteroids. Watch out! Ka-blam!

Mega Brain

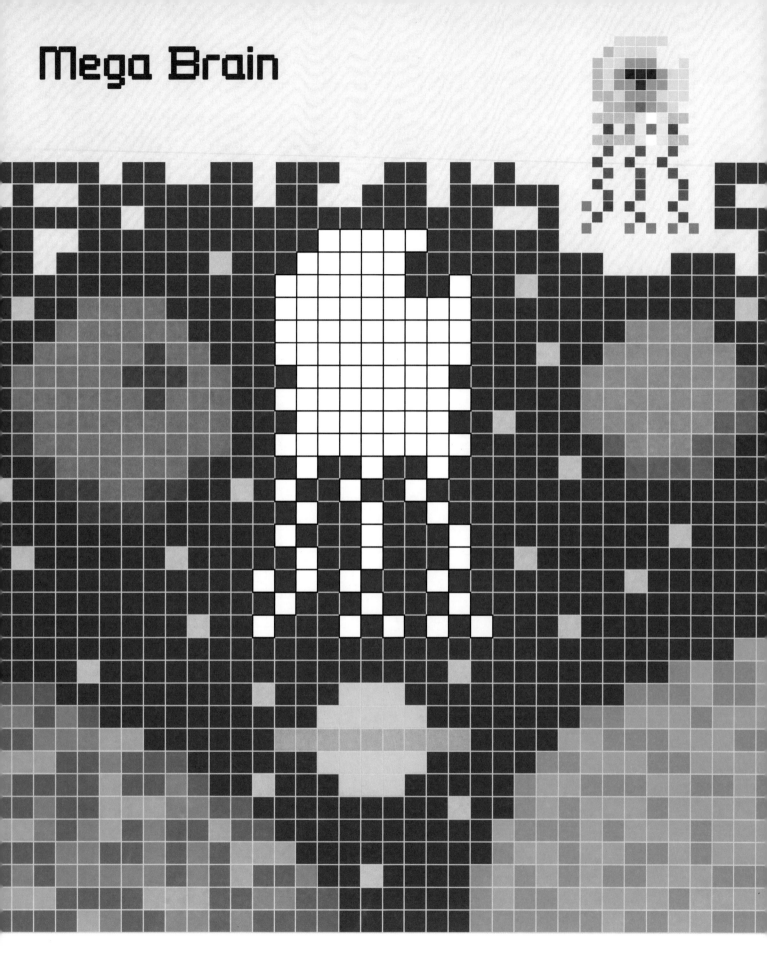

An extraterrestrial brain fitted to a robotic body, Mega Brain comes from the Plexsus Nebula in search of a new home. Bzzzzzzz!

Captain Chaos

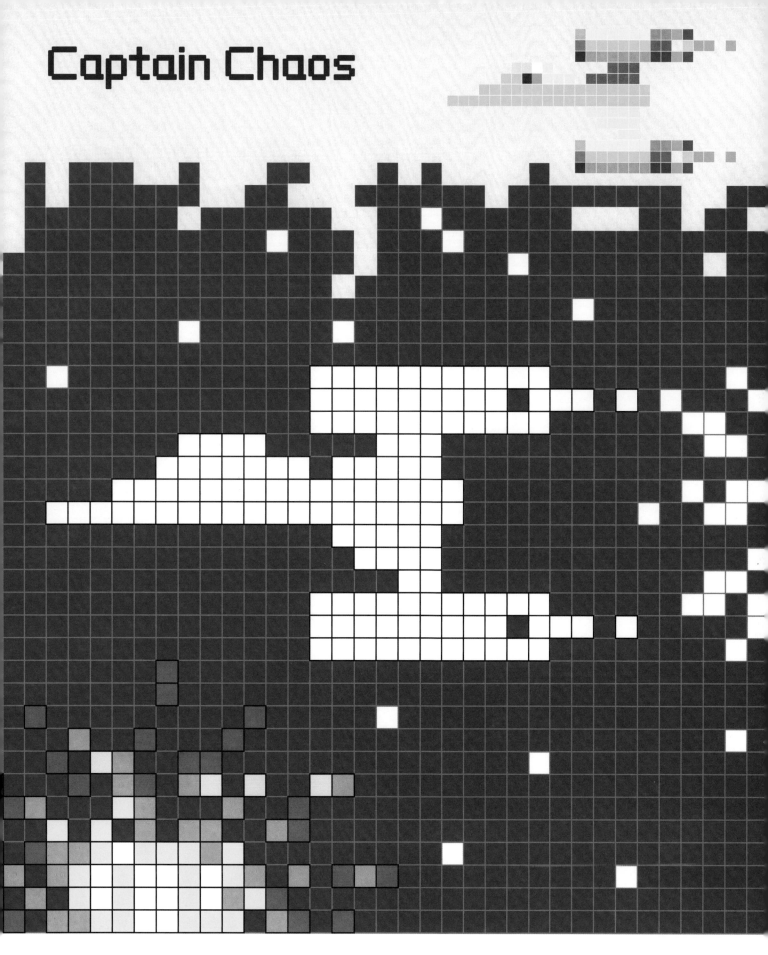

I'm a deep space flying ace in my supersonic fighter. I keep the galaxy safe from invaders by blasting them to smithereens. Take that!

Solar Sailor

Ahoy there! My craft is powered by solar rays. It's slow to accelerate but can reach enormous speeds.

Space Pirate

Space pirates roam the galaxy looking for unarmed ships to attack.
Warp the plank!

Neutreno

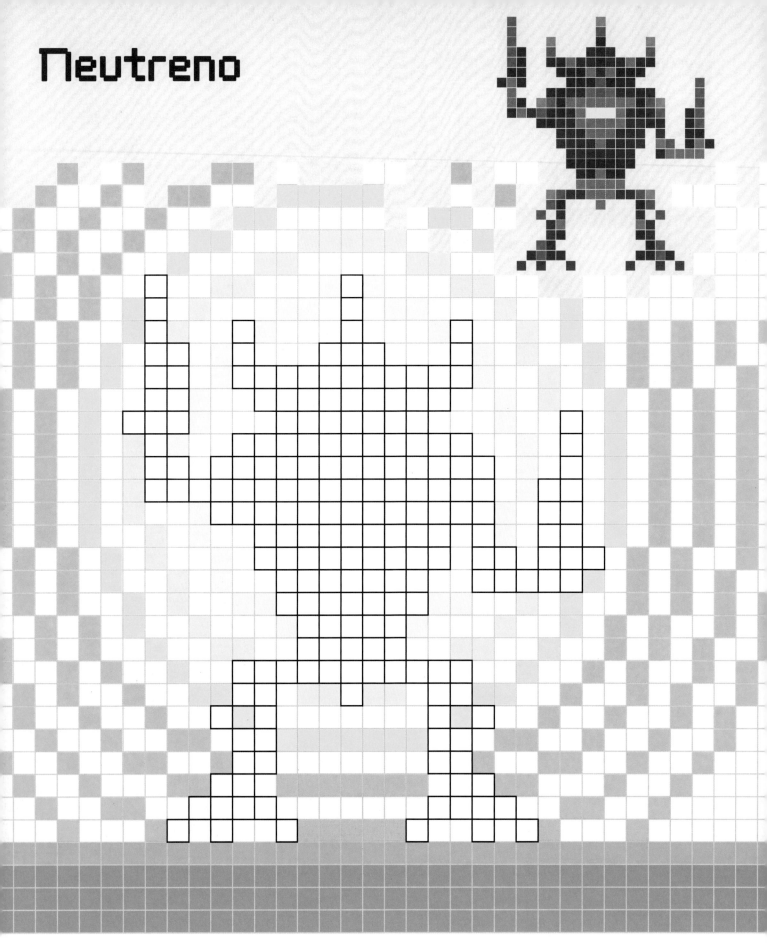

Neutreno is the super-intelligent leader of an alien alliance from the edge of the Basmat system...prepare to meet your maker, earthling!

Rocket

3...2...1...Lift off! In the distant future, some people like to fly rockets from the ancient past. This 21st century rocket is so old-fashioned!

Battle Droids

Destroy! Destroy! Battle Droids roam the galaxy destroying any threat to the Galactic Empire.

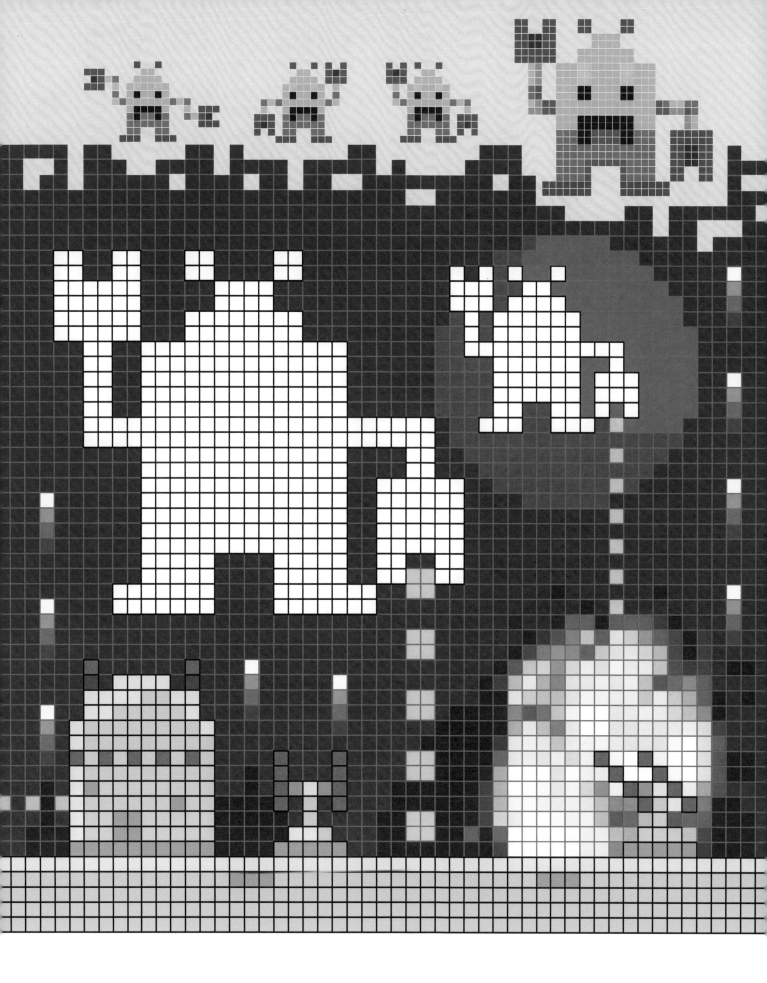

Arachnid

Dinner time! Arachnid is a massive eight-legged alien that lives in outer space. He catches his prey in enormous space webs.

Bounty Hunter

Surrender, scum! Bounty Hunter will work for anyone that pays! His laser gun and rocket boots make him a deadly enemy.

The Blip

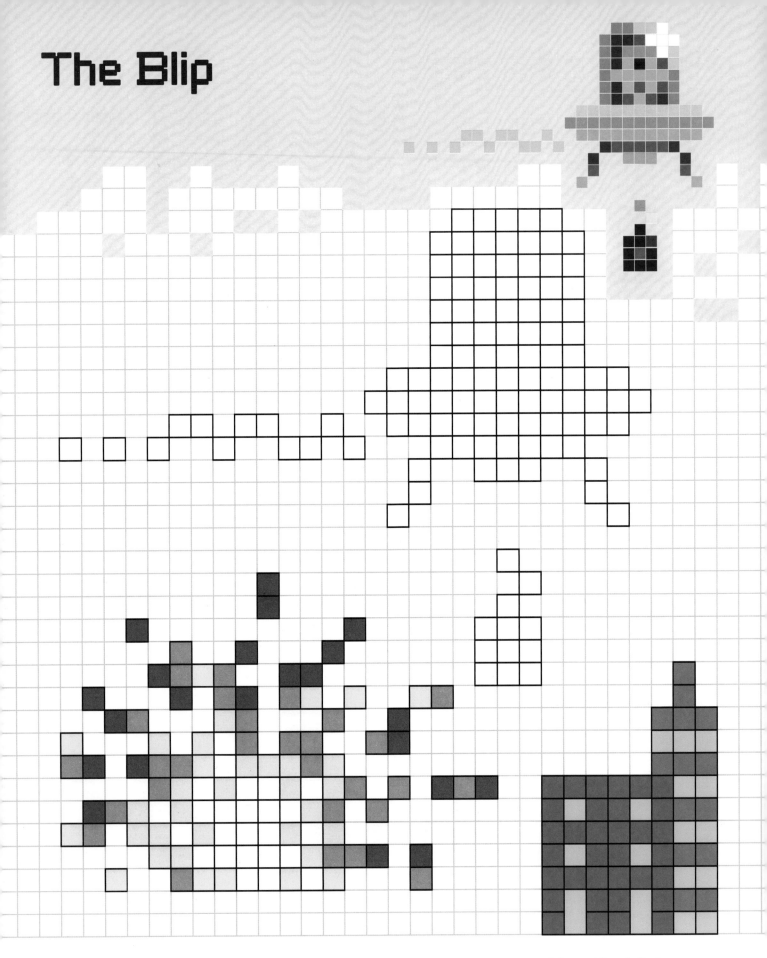

Blip...blip...BOOM! I'm just a blip on your screen—an unidentified flying object. I whizz through space, looking for new civilizations...to destroy!

Starsuit

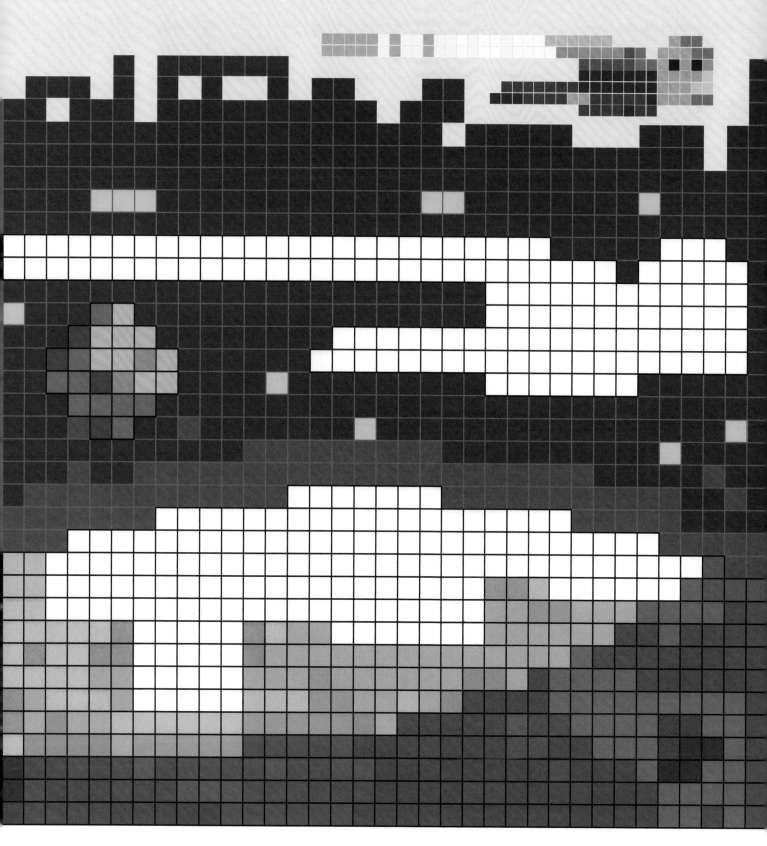

Maximum speed! A starsuit is a special spacesuit that can fly short distances through space. It looks like this guy is in a hurry!

Rampaging Robot

Beep, beep, beep! This huge robot has gone on the rampage! It's destroying everything in its way with its red laser-beam eyes!

Apocalypse

Apocalypse's asteroid home was destroyed by a rogue mining craft. Now he's sworn to destroy the galaxy! Mwa ha ha!

Interceptor

I'm called out when an unidentified ship is spotted. My ship is fast and well-armed and I mean business! State your name and purpose!

Lord Blob

Lord Blob has declared war on the Star Council. Things could get nasty!
Bow down to your new lord!

Incoming!

The Space Station is picking up a number of unidentified flying objects.
They're not slowing down, Captain! Bleep, bleep, bleep!

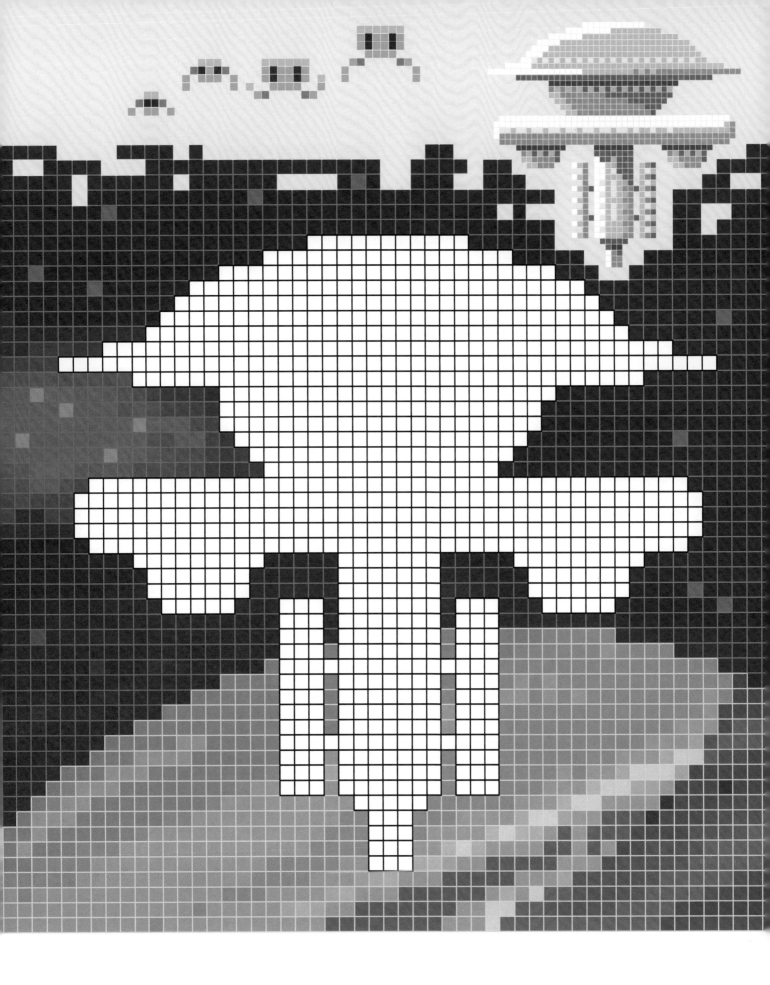

Space Station Command

This is the captain speaking...the Space Station is under attack!
All crew report to positions! Repeat, all crew report to positions!

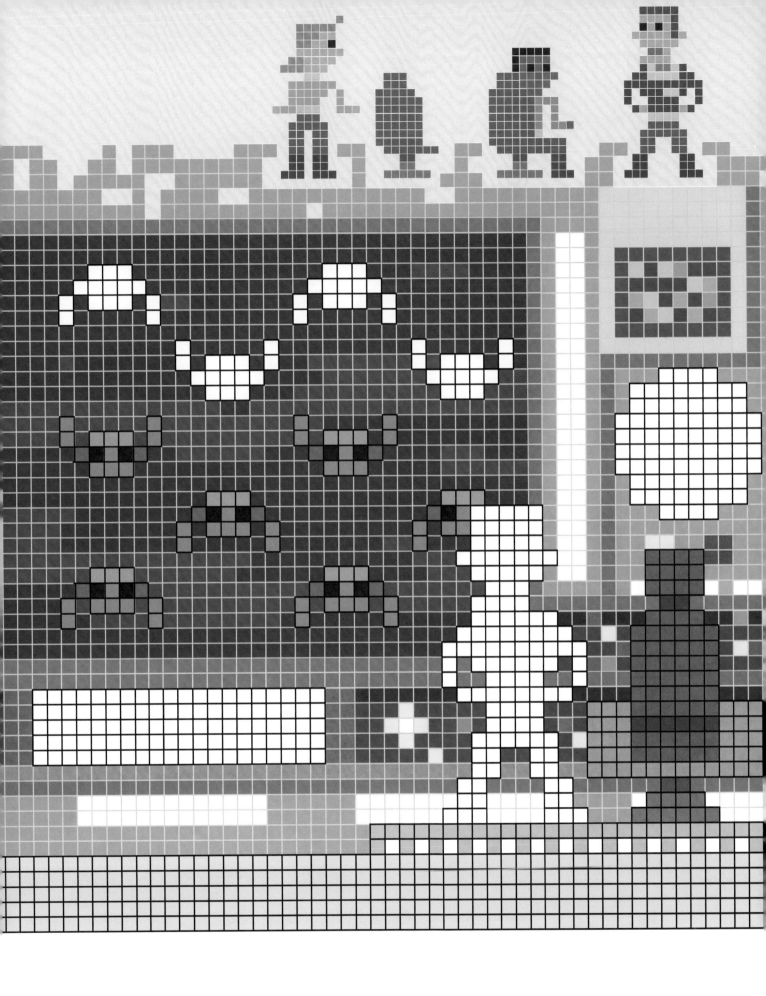

Scramble Fighters

The Space Station fighter craft have been scrambled to meet the attack,
but they are heavily outnumbered.

Star Tanks

The Space Station only has a few star tanks and they are very slow, but their laser cannons pack a powerful punch. Blam! Blam! Blam!

Destroyer

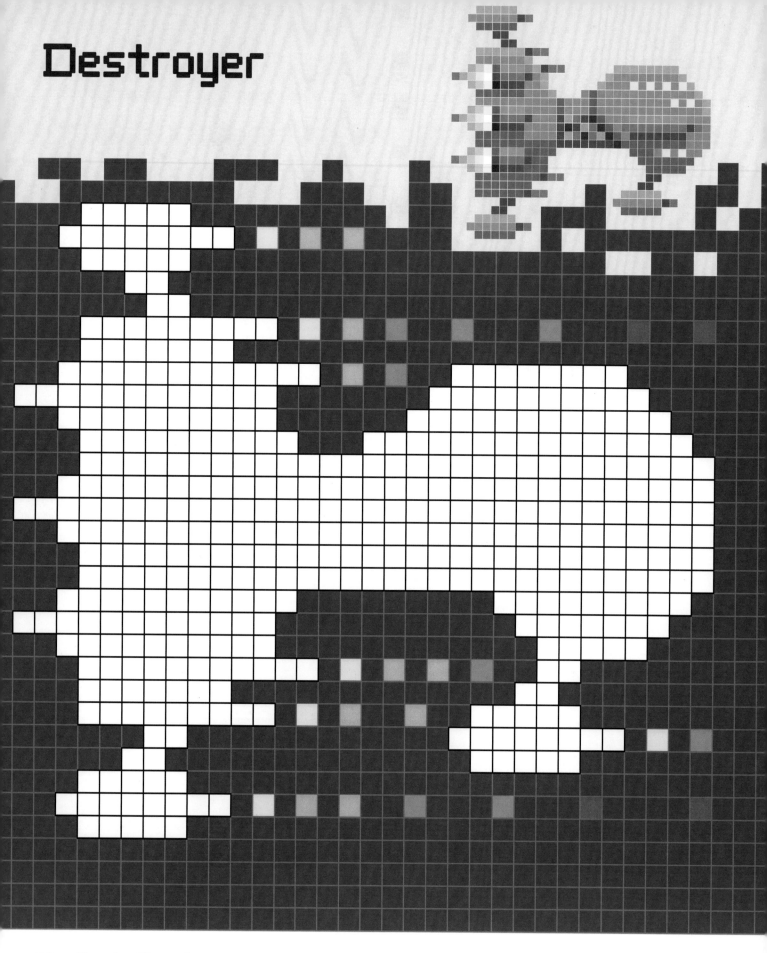

The Battle Fleet is on its way! This massive destroyer is leading the fleet into the battle. Surrender or be destroyed!

Troop Carrier

When the Battle Fleet needs to transport troopers, it uses these enormous carrier vessels. All troops report to the loading bay!

Space Battle

The Space Station fighters are desperately holding back the Blob attack.
Pow! Pow! Zap! Zap! Pow!

Victory

The Battle Fleet troops arrived and defeated Lord Blob's army. But nobody has spotted Lord Blob fleeing to safety. Next time, earthlings!

Mongo the Merciless

Mongo the Merciless has captured a lost fighter craft, and now he's started to eat it! Munch, munch!

Moondusa

On the dark side of a small moon lives someone you really don't want to meet! Moondusa and her terrifying space-snake hair! Sssss!

Escape Pod

Aiiiieeeeeeeee! When my ship malfunctioned I had to escape in this tiny escape pod. Now I'm re-entering the atmosphere of the planet Xantar.

Galumph

Galumph is the biggest life form ever discovered. He floats through space eating asteroids and small moons. Chomp, chomp!

Spaceship "X"

Spaceship "X" is the Battle Fleet's top-secret new craft. It's powered by thought and can travel instantly across the universe. Hold tight!

Meteor Shower

Hold on! This planet is being hit by flying space rocks! You can feel the impacts from here!

Spaceship Repair

This spaceship has hit some space junk and needs urgent repairs before it can continue. Clunk! Clunk!

Space Dragons

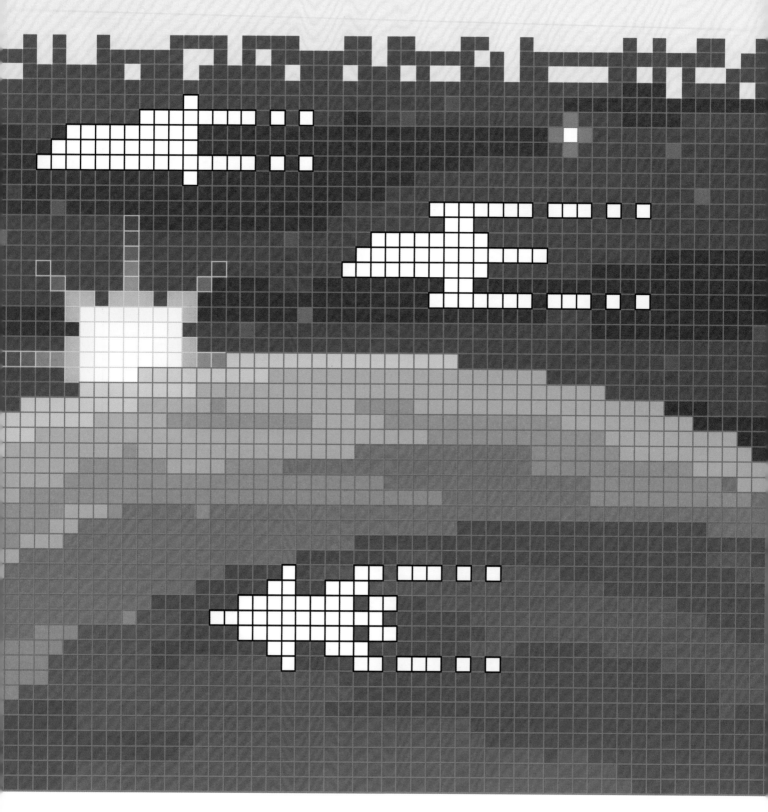

Uh-oh! Don't look now, but there seem to be some space dragons behind us. Hopefully they're not hungry!

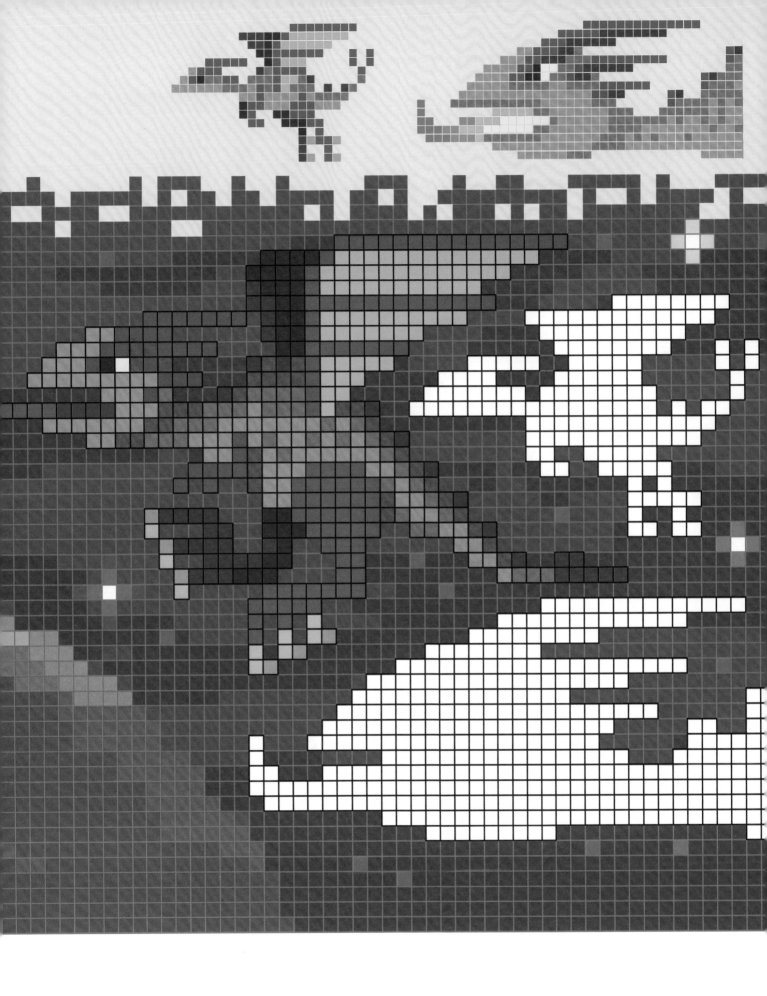

Infantry Droid

Infantry droids are the Battle Fleet's shock troops. They can fight in any environment and they never give up. Zap! Zap! Whirr...Zap!

Vampoid

Vampoid stalks the dark edge of the solar system, looking for prey.

Shoot Out!

Lord Blob has been found, and infantry droids have been sent to take him captive. But his Blobbiness won't come without a fight! Ka-pow! Ka-pow!

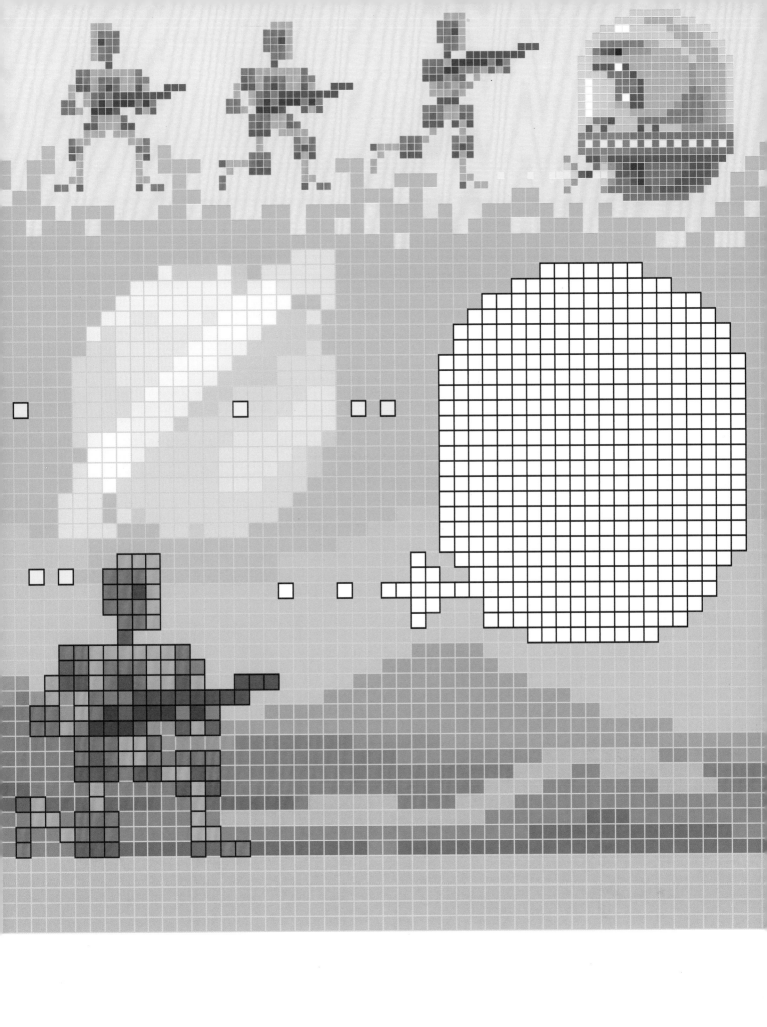

Fly Past

The galaxy is safe again! There's a triumphant fly past of Battle Fleet
ships! Hip hip hooray!